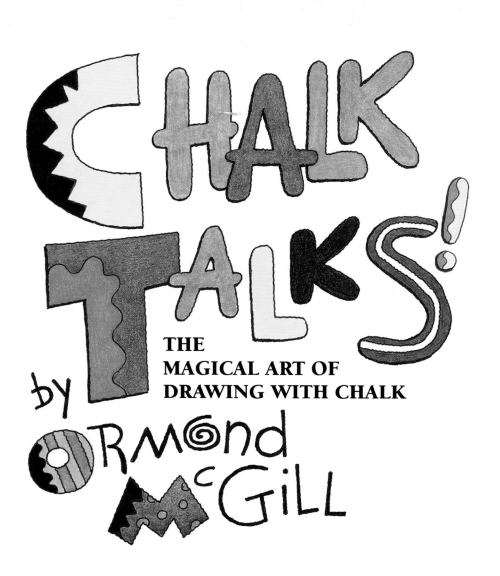

CHALK TALKS!

THE MAGICAL ART OF DRAWING WITH CHALK

by ORMOND McGILL

**Drawings by
Anne Canevari Green**

The Millbrook Press
Brookfield, Connecticut

*This book is dedicated to the memory of Harlan Tarbell—
master magician, teacher, and artist—who brought
joy to the hearts of all in audiences throughout the world.*

Published by The Millbrook Press, Inc.
2 Old New Milford Road, Brookfield, Connecticut 06804

Library of Congress Cataloging-in-Publication Data
McGill, Ormond.
Chalk talks : the magical art of drawing with chalk / by Ormond
McGill ; drawings by Anne Canevari Green.
p.   cm.
Includes bibliographical references and index.
Summary: Describes how to present chalk talks, just as the artist
and magician Harlan Tarbell performed them on stage, using a
drawing board, an easel, paper, chalk, or a felt-tipped marker,
and imagination.
ISBN 1-56294-669-2 (lib. bdg.)
1. Chalk talks—Juvenile literature.   2. Tarbell, Harlan, 1890–
1960—Juvenile literature.   [1. Drawing—Technique.   2. Chalk.
3. Tarbell, Harlan, 1890–1960.]   I. Green, Anne Canevari, ill.
II. Title.
NC865.M35   741.2'3—dc20   95-1952   CIP   AC

CONTENTS

PREFACE

This book teaches art through the art in magic. It shows you how to draw in ways that work like magic and how to entertain with your magical art.

Chalk Talks! was inspired by the remarkable work of Dr. Harlan Tarbell, who died several decades ago. During his lifetime, Harlan Tarbell was recognized as an outstanding magical performer, as an instructor to great magicians around the world, and as an artist of distinction. He combined his artistic skill with magic to produce the now famous entertainment known as the Tarbell Chalk Talks.

This book is a memorial to this great magician and artist.

Ormond McGill

Tips for the Performer

Here are the ingredients for success as a performance artist. You have to do more than produce good art. You have to entertain your audience at the same time. What makes Chalk Talk easy to do is that your pictures will be judged not by how well you draw but by how clever you are when you draw. Keep the following dozen tips in mind when you perform the Chalk Talks in this book.

1. *Personality.* Personality is so important for an entertainer! Be alive and vital. Put snap into your work. Make the audience like you.

2. *Showmanship.* When you draw in front of an audience, make every line and movement count. Be open in your work so your spectators can appreciate your skill. When you have to be secretive, cover yourself in a natural way so the audience will not

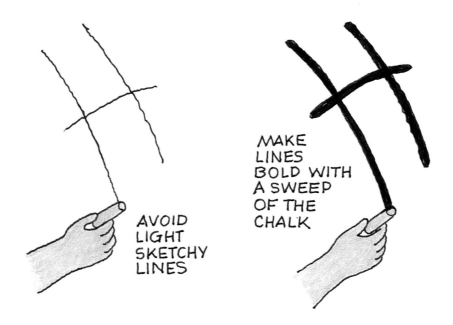

AVOID LIGHT SKETCHY LINES

MAKE LINES BOLD WITH A SWEEP OF THE CHALK

be suspicious. An important part of magical showmanship is to direct your spectators to see what you want them to see and to draw their attention away from what you want to hide.

3. *Rough sketches.* To develop confidence and smoothness in performing Chalk Talk (especially the first time you practice this art), make light sketches of the various pictures you will draw later on. The large sheets of newsprint paper you will be using are beige. When you outline your drawings with a hard lead pencil, the faint lines will be invisible to your audience but not to you.

All you have to do is cover the pencil lines with chalk when you draw. Later, as you gain experience, you can do without these guidelines, but at first they will be a great help to you.

4. *Drawing position.* Work from the side of the easel so the audience can see the paper. People like to watch your art unfold.

WORK FROM THE SIDE
SO AUDIENCE CAN SEE
WHAT IT'S ALL ABOUT

AVOID STANDING IN
FRONT OF BOARD AND
OBSTRUCTING THE VIEW

5. *The dramatic pause.* After drawing a picture, pause a moment so the spectators will have time to appreciate its significance. This is called a dramatic pause. It should not be too long or too short. Proper timing is important to good theater. Allow just enough time for the audience to understand what you have done.

6. *Follow-through.* Each time you complete a drawing, remove it from the pad and place it on a table or on the floor beside your easel. You can tell your audience that some of the pictures will be given away after the show. You will have a mad scramble on your hands. Remember to treat each drawing you make with respect. It is a work of art.

7. *A touch of mystery.* These drawings have a touch of mystery, so when you place them aside be careful not to expose

any modus operandi. As a good magician always does, keep your secrets to yourself.

8. *Variety.* Put plenty of variety in it. Your act is called a routine, and a good routine makes good theater.

9. *Keeping up with the times.* We live in a busy time and public interests change constantly. Pay attention to the news and from time to time make a comment about an up-to-date topic. Art might be timeless, but making yours contemporary will add sparkle to your show.

10. *Rehearsal.* Rehearse every detail of your show before you present it. Learn your drawings and your patter lines so well that they become second nature. And use special care to keep your program a good length. Never bore your audience; always maintain their enthusiasm. Learn to stop drawing at the exact moment when interest has reached its peak.

11. *Musical background.* If possible, have music playing in the background while you draw. Music gives a rhythm to things and keeps them moving. Place a cassette player on the stage or on a table near your easel. Plan your music in advance so each piece fits the mood of your drawing. Start a new piece of music each time you begin to draw. When you complete a drawing, stop the music, display the picture, and accept your applause.

12. *The big picture.* Chalk Talk is an art form that magicians perform on a stage. But you can stage your own performance pretty much anywhere—at home, in an auditorium, or in a classroom. When you do the magical Chalk Talks, just be sure you stand at a distance from your audience. Don't let them see what you're really doing!

The more carefully you plan your program, the more successful you will be. Plan your program well. Know exactly what you are going to do and do it expertly.

Always remember that in show business it is not so much what you do as how you do it.

Get Ready to Chalk Talk

It is amazing how people will stand around and watch an artist draw. Art holds a fascination all its own. You will experience this as you draw, and so will your friends as they watch you perform. It is quite remarkable how just a few simple drawn lines can tell a story.

The apparatus required for a Chalk Talk act is quite simple and can be found at any art supply store. All you need is an easel to hold your drawing board, paper, and chalk or a felt-tipped marker. You can even do without an easel. Just ask someone to come up and hold your drawing board for you while you talk with your chalk. People like to do this.

You will need a pad of print stock, 26 by 43 inches (66 by 109 centimeters). This size works well because you can draw large enough pictures for even a big audience to see.

To draw, you can use either of two materials: felt-tipped markers or chalk sticks. When Harlan Tarbell was in show business, felt-tipped markers did not exist. He used large, black chalk sticks, called lecturer's chalk. Although you can still find chalk sticks in most art supply stores, they are not very popular today. They are messy to work with and leave chalk dust on your hands and on the floor. If you choose to use chalk sticks, be sure to place a drop cloth on the floor to protect rugs or carpeting.

You will probably find it easier to produce the broad strokes of Tarbell's Chalk Talks with thick felt-tipped markers. They should be water soluble, though. Both the markers and the chalk sticks come in many colors. You might want to have a few colors on hand to add interest to your show.

Start your Chalk Talk act by telling the audience that you are going to draw pictures that tell a story, that you will draw them with the fewest lines possible, and that you will make ten drawings in ten minutes. (Actually you will probably take longer, but the spectators will become so interested that they will not challenge how much time you take, and a remark like this keys them up to see something unusual.)

Chalk Talk drawings, for the more part, consist of entertaining transformation pictures (in which one picture turns into another) and upside-downside pictures (in which a drawing seen one way shows something entirely different when it is turned over). Novelty pictures—for example, drawings formed from a person's name—are another way to entertain with chalk. Harlan Tarbell, a magician as well as an artist, even put a touch of magic into some of his drawings. His magical Chalk Talks would do mystifying things, leaving his spectators puzzled and intrigued.

Chalk Talk calls for a bit of patter to set the idea of the drawings for the audience, either before or during the drawing. Keep it to a minimum, and let the drawings, more or less, speak for themselves. That is why this art form is called Chalk Talk. Tarbell himself often presented his patter in rhymes. These rhymes will be included with some of the drawings. The use of rhyme, of course, is optional, but it does add an artistic touch.

Many of Tarbell's Chalk Talk drawings have become standards to this form of entertaining with art.

Now on to some original Tarbell art. . . .

part 1

ENTERTAINING CHALK TALKS

Starting the Show

Your show is ready to start when your props are all set and your easel stands center stage. You come on, and your first task is to capture the attention of your audience. Here's a bit of humorous patter to get things started:

Get ready for some magical fun with drawing. It is called Chalk Talk. Magic is fun to watch. Drawing is fun to watch. Together, they are the most fun of all. Let's start by producing a magician.

Which is the most popular magic trick in the world? You all know what it is: producing a rabbit from a top hat.

So, let's draw a top hat and then show the rabbit coming out of the hat.

Draw a top hat, and then a rabbit coming out of the hat. Continue your patter:

Well, we've got the rabbit. Now we've got to find the magician.

Take the drawing off the board, turn it upside down, and replace it on the pad.

Complete the picture as shown, and say with a flourish:

There he is: THE MAGICIAN!

Transformation Pictures

Transformation pictures will add to your repertoire and give variety to your shows. Draw each of them, as shown in the sets of figures 1 through 4 on the following pages. Tarbell has supplied a little rhyme for each patter.

      In Chalk Talk the patter must fit the drawing as a unit. You can start drawing,

            then talk,

                    then draw some more,

                          and then talk again.

      In presenting transformation pictures, you should start talking after you draw the first figure. Then draw figures 2 and 3, and complete the rhyme as you step aside and show the completed picture of figure 4.

Fresh Fish

Set aside your opening drawing. Fresh Fish makes a good second drawing for your act. Turn to the audience and say:

Often a Chalk Talk picture tells its own story, so no words of explanation are necessary. Here is one I call Fresh Fish. I am sure you will get the idea.

Step up to the board and draw a fish, as shown in illustration 1. Then boldly print the word FISH under it. Step aside and let the audience see what you have done.

Now complete the drawing (steps 2 through 4). Again move aside, and for the pantomime ending add the word FRESH.

Pause a moment to let the idea sink home. Then, with flare, add an exclamation mark.

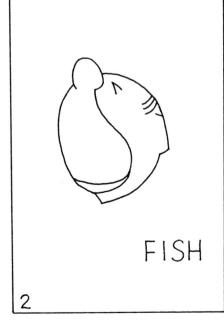

Remove the picture from the easel and hold it up to give the audience one last look, then go on with the show.

The Monkey and the Cat

Here's a Tarbell original along with his patter in rhyme.

Ladies and gentlemen, here's a drawing I believe you will find interesting. I will describe it to you, as it proceeds along, in a bit of rhyme. I call it The Monkey and the Cat.

Step up to the drawing board and draw a monkey on a fence, as shown in figure 1 on the next page. Then recite:

Upon a fence a monkey stood,
Just as a monkey sometimes would:
To sing and dance, and chin and chat
To a friend of his, a nearby cat.

When you complete the rhyme, turn again to the drawing board, and transform the monkey into a cat, as shown in figures 2, 3, and 4. The picture "talks" for itself.

Remove the drawing. Show it to your audience, and put it aside. Go on to the next.

The Dutch Boy's Windmill

The windmill's wheel goes round and round
By it a farmer's wheat is ground.
As it turns it gives much joy
To little Hans, the miller's boy.

As Grandpa Tells It

When my grandpa was a little boy
A lot of hair grew on his head;
But now it's walked down to his chin;
At least that's what my grandpa said.

The Lady and the Mouse

Once upon a time there was a mouse
Who called upon a dear old lady's house.
Indeed it was just a friendly call:
A chair, a scream, and that was all.

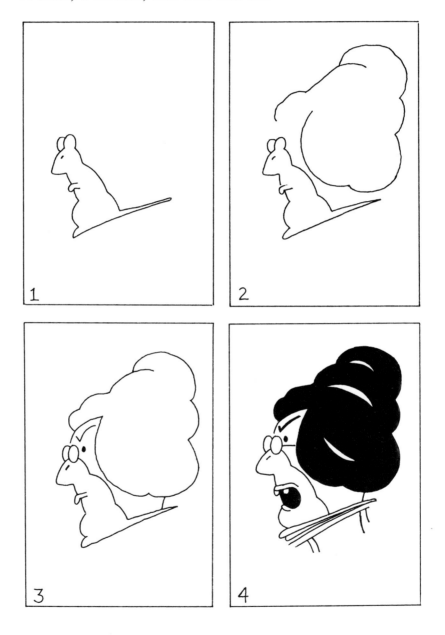

The Funny Magic Bunny

Every magician has a bunny
That he feeds on milk and honey.
But as it is a magic bunny
It always acts kind of funny.
For this tricky little rabbit
Has an aggravating habit
Of turning into something else
When the magician tries to grab it.

When Towser Ate the Mouse

A mouse who lived in an empty flat
Said, "Gosh, I ought to live forever.
No dog or cat can ever get me,
For I am much too clever!"
A puppy spied the little mouse.
He's what breeders call a mouser.
Here's Towser now inside the house,
And here's the mouse inside of Towser.

Is It a Bird? Is It a Man?

[Draw 1] *Is this a bird? Yes, this is a bird.*
A black bird with white wings.
The bird is sitting on a limb

[Draw 2] *Whose leaves formed a canopy over him.*

[Draw 3] *And this is the man*
Who laughed at the bird
Who sat on the limb

[Draw 4] *Whose leaves formed a canopy over him.*

The Scarecrow

[Draw 1] *I've tried and tried to keep this crow*
        Away from my garden patch.
        He eats my lettuce and my kale;
        His wits I cannot match.
        At last I've found a qualified man
        Who will guard my garden night and day.
        He may be only made of straw,
        But he'll keep that crow away! [Draw 2, 3, 4]

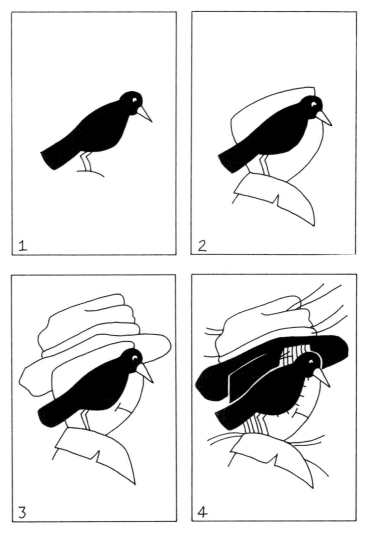

The Bewitching Dove

[Draw the witch as in figure 1.]

> *It looks like I have drawn a witch,*
> *And seeing is believing.*
> *But just watch me finish this,*
> *And see how Chalk Talks are deceiving.*
>
> *Hocus-Pocus! I add this line*
> *And then another just above.*

[Draw figures 2 and 3.]

> *Here's a curve, and there you are!*
> *The witch has turned into a dove.*

[Complete the drawing, as in figure 4.]

The Lion Tamer

Here's a good finale for your transformation pictures.

Say to your audience:

Here's a fellow I call the Lion Tamer. I will draw him for you.

Draw this picture:

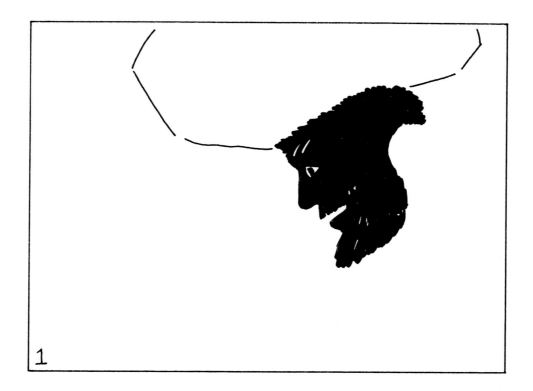

When you're done, look at the audience, raise your eyebrows, and ask:

Why do I call him the Lion Tamer? (Pause.) *Here's why!*

Complete the drawing as shown above, turning the lion tamer into a lion.

Your drawing has answered the question.

UPSIDE-DOWN PICTURES

It's time in your show to do something different. Let's try an upside-down picture. When you show your audience what appears to be a finished picture and then turn it over to show them an entirely different one, the effect is quite amazing. Now pick up the chalk and patter:

Ladies and gentlemen, for my next Chalk Talk I am going to draw one of those weird characters that are so popular these days in science-fiction movies. I call this monster the God of the Sea.

You proceed to draw the creature shown in figure 1 on the following page.

After completing the drawing, step aside and say:

This, ladies and gentlemen, is the God of the Sea. In case you are wondering why he is called this, I will show you.

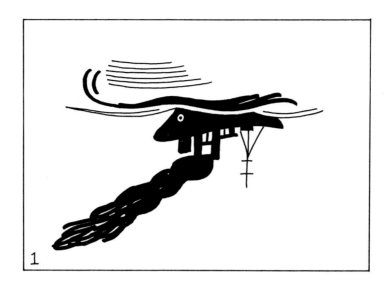

Remove the drawing from your easel, turn it upside down, and put it back on the easel (figure 2). Stand in front of the picture while you put it in place, but make it clear to your audience that you are turning the picture over. Then step aside and let the impact of the ship sailing the high seas hit the crowd.

The drawing speaks for itself, and you will get a nice hand. Remove and show it; then put it aside.

On the following pages are several upside-down pictures designed by Tarbell. This first one is a classic:

The Woman and the Grouchy Clown

This is one of the most famous upside-down pictures. Viewed this side up you see a young woman. Turn it over and you see a grouchy old clown.

The Elephant and the Ostrich

Here's another upside-down picture. While drawing figures 1, 2, and 3, you patter to your audience about a trip to the circus:

I was looking at an elephant, when the most incredible thing happened!

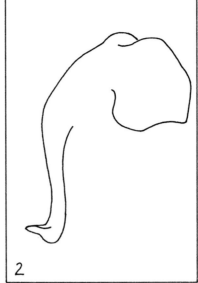

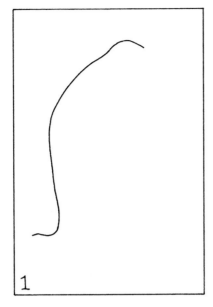

Turn the picture over and say:

> *Right before my eyes, he turned into an ostrich!*

Your audience will see figure 4.

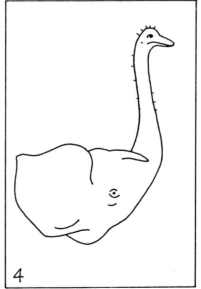

Dad and the Baby Buggy

Draw the baby buggy shown in figure 1 below while pattering this verse:

When Daddy wheels this carriage out,
The old-time friends he meets will shout,
"Hey, Bill, old top! I wish you joy!
What's in the buggy? Girl or boy?"

Then Dad yells, "Both," and shouts with glee.
When each one asks, "How can that be?"
He lifts the carriage robe and grins,
And answers, "How? Because they're twins!"

Complete the drawing, as in figures 2 and 3.

Turn figure 3 over and you have the proud daddy shown in figure 4.

Cupid and the Stork

Here's a cute upside-down picture to perform for a family crowd.

Draw Cupid, symbol of love, as in figures 1, 2, and 3. Cupid carries a heart and his arrows.

Turn figure 3 over and he is transformed into a stork carrying a precious bundle of joy (see figure 4).

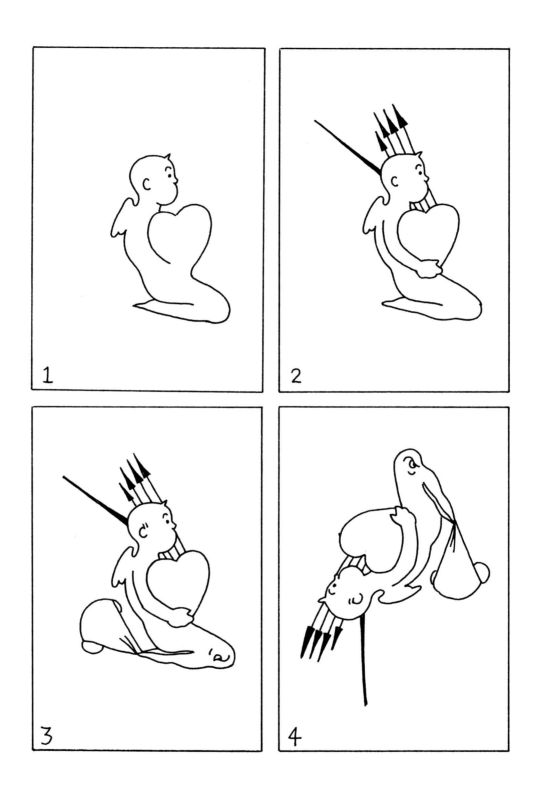

part 2

novelty chalk talks

WHAT'S in A NAME?

To put some novelty in your Chalk Talk act ask a girl in the audience to call out her first name. Suppose her name is June.

Write it boldly on the drawing board:

Look at the name for a moment or two, and scratch your head as though you were trying to figure out what to do with it. Then start drawing and turn the name into a portrait of a June bride.

With a little practice you can draw a portrait of a boy or girl around any name you hear.

The examples using the names Alice and Frank will give you an idea of what you can do.

Try to see how many drawings you can make from your own name.

A Number-One Student

Using the numbers as shown on the next page, you begin the figures of a boy going to school. Then, use these numbers to complete the drawing of a boy.

Progress through figures 2 and 3, and end up with figure 4.

You have a baseball umpire making a call at a game.

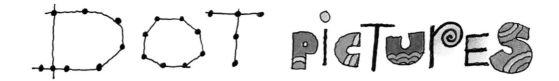

DOT PICTURES

Making dot pictures lets you use your artistic imagination. Tell your audience that you will create a drawing based on a random arrangement of dots.

Have someone from the audience come forward and place dots on the paper, in any way he or she chooses. Figure 1 is just one example of how the dots might be arranged.

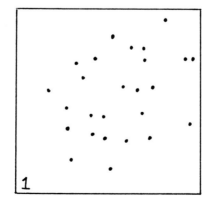

It looks difficult but it's really simple. Just use your artistic skill. No matter how complicated the arangements of dots, you can always form something from them, such as a cute little kitten playing with a ball of yarn (see figure 2).

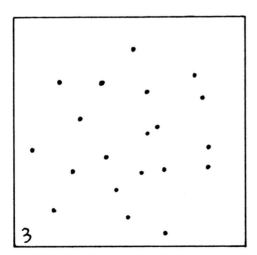

Figure 3 is another example of the dots someone from the audience might place on the paper. A drawing that could be made from those dots is shown in figure 4.

Using the dots to form a landscape is another good idea, as shown here in figures 5 and 6.

The secret of creating successful dot pictures is that while the audience thinks the performer uses the dots as points to form the picture, actually you simply manage to pass through them while completing whatever drawing you have in mind. The possibilities are really endless!

Circle, Square, Triangle

Audiences love to see creative talent in operation. Here is another way to show it:

Draw a circle, a triangle, and a square on your paper.

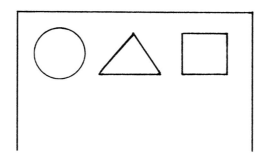

Then have someone come up and draw an arrangement of these shapes in any way he or she pleases. Figures 1 and 3 show examples. Figures 2 and 4 show how these are used to form elements of a picture.

Figures 5, 6, 7, and 8 show some more drawings that were made using the circle, square, and triangle as creative elements. However they are placed, you can form them into a picture.

No one in America is more famous than George Washington or Abraham Lincoln.

Practice drawing these historic figures until you feel confident that you have captured them. Then you are ready to turn their portraits into an effective Chalk Talk stunt.

Here's the Stunt

Ask two people to stand on either side of your easel. One holds a one-dollar bill with the picture of George Washington. The other holds a five-dollar bill with the picture of Abraham Lincoln.

As you draw the portraits of these famous men from memory, keep glancing at the bills as though you were reproducing the faces directly from the bills. Your audience will be doubly impressed!

Figures 1, 2, 3, and 4 show you
a simple way to draw our first president.

Figures 5, 6, 7, and 8 do
the same for "Honest Abe."

part 3

MAGICAL CHALK TALKS

On occasion, Harlan Tarbell would add magic to his art.

Here are some clever tricks you can do.
They will take practice, but don't get discouraged!

Just follow my instructions step by step, and
rehearse your performance with care.

The Vanishing Chalk Line

The secret of this trick is that you pick up the chalk (or marker) and seem to draw a line on the paper with it. But you are actually bringing down a length of black tape on the board by pulling it through the board and paper. To your audience the tape looks quite like a chalk line. To make the line vanish, all you have to do is pull the tape back behind the board with your left hand.

The illustration on the next page shows how you attach the tape to the back of your board and then pull it through a hole and back again to trick your audience.

Fasten one end of the tape to the back of the drawing board with a thumbtack. Push the other end through a hole in the board, then through a small slit you have cut in the paper. Make sure that the tip pokes through the board so you can grasp it when you perform the trick. It is a good idea to cover the tip of the black tape with a little slip of paper that matches the pad. That way, your audience won't suspect a thing!

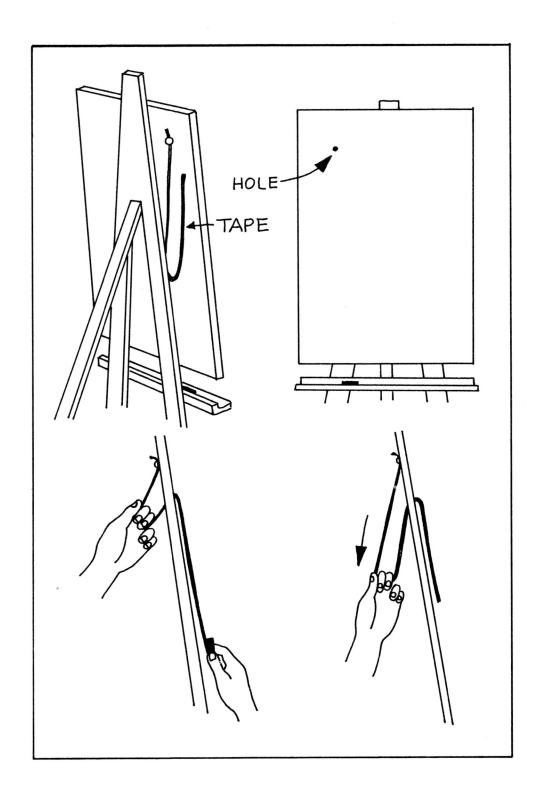

HOLE

TAPE

To do the trick, pick up a piece of black chalk (or a black marker). Face the audience and patter in a serious voice:

The first thing an artist must learn is to draw a straight line.

Then turn to the board, and pretend to place the chalk on the paper. What you really do is grasp the end of the tape with the fingers holding the chalk, and pull it down. The chalk is held away from the paper a little, but the black tape pulled down looks like a straight black line that you have really drawn.

Stand aside, let the audience see the bold line, and say:

Of course that line rather messes up the paper for further drawing, so I'd better make it disappear. Watch it go.

With your left hand behind the board, pull the tape back until it vanishes through the slit.

The line you have "drawn" seems to disappear right before their eyes!

THE LEMON from NOWHERE

You will need a yellow marker for this trick.

Begin by drawing a lemon, as shown in figure 1.

Now place your hand over it to pluck it from the board, as shown in figure 2.

Your lemon drawing has disappeared, and, as you can see in figure 3, you are holding a real lemon in your hand.

Magic!

Figures 4, 5, 6, and 7 show you how to perform the trick. Cut one vertical slit in your paper and two small diagonal ones. Run a strip of paper through the large slit. See figure 4. (The strip should match the paper of your drawing pad.) Tuck the strip of paper into the diagonal slits to hold it in place. See figure 5. This strip needs to be large enough to frame a drawing of a full-size lemon.

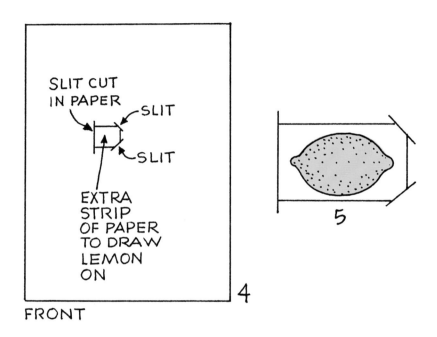

Figure 6 shows the back of your paper. Paste an envelope just to the side of the vertical slit so you can slide the strip of paper into it. Run a thread through the end of the strip, so you can pull it back when you want to. If you tie a paper clip to the free end of the thread, you will have a handy little handle. When you pull the clip, the strip of paper (which will contain your drawing of the lemon) moves from the front of the pad, through the slit, and into the envelope behind. Your drawing of the lemon will disappear and leave the surface of the paper blank.

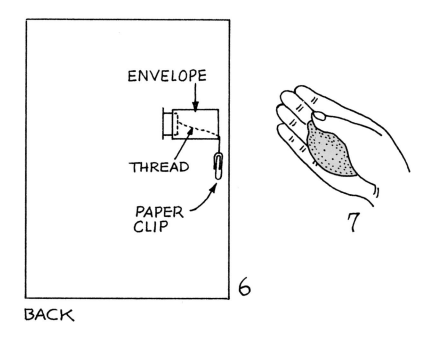

BACK

The real lemon is on your drawing tray ready for you to palm (conceal in the palm of your hand) when you need to. Here goes the performance:

Draw a lemon on the prepared strip with yellow chalk. Place the chalk on the tray and palm the lemon in your right hand, as shown in figure 7. Keep the back of your hand to the audience so no one can see the lemon.

Bring your right hand, with the palmed lemon, in front of the drawing of the lemon, simultaneously pulling on the paper clip that pulls the strip through the slip and into the envelope on the back of the paper. Press the real lemon against the paper, allowing a bit of it to show above your hand. It appears to be part of your drawing. Then pluck it fully off the pad and exhibit it as a real lemon to the audience. Toss it to someone.

Surprise! The pad is blank so you can use it for your next Lemon From Nowhere chalk talk. The following transformation picture fits in nicely with this Chalk Talk.

Draw three yellow lemons on your pad. Then take your black chalk and turn the lemons into characters like the ones shown below. Lemon 1 becomes a woman with a bun. Lemon 2 becomes a turtle and Lemon 3 a nervous batter waiting for the pitch.

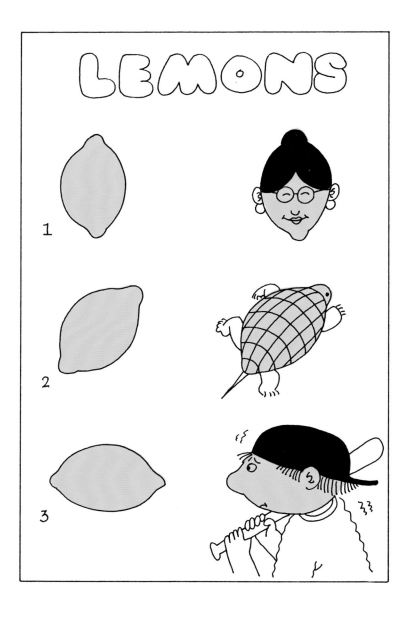

THE MAGIC BANANA

The Magic Banana is similar to the Lemon From Nowhere, but in this trick you draw a stalk of bananas and pull a real banana from the drawing.

The illustrations below show how you prepare the magic for this easy but effective stunt.

First, straighten out a paper clip and bend both ends into hooks. Attach one of these hooks to a real banana. Then sew a little ring inside your coat where you can hook the banana conveniently with the other end of your paper clip so you can get it when you want it. See figures 1 and 2.

To draw a stalk of bananas, smear some yellow chalk on the paper in a silhouette of a bunch of bananas (figure 3). Then, with black chalk, draw in the bananas on the stalk (figure 4).

While you are drawing, stand in front of the stalk. When you are nearly finished, secretly remove the real banana from your jacket and hook it on the drawn bunch in the center of the middle row. The real banana will blend in with the drawing.

Place some finishing touches on your drawing. When it is completed, surprise the audience by reaching up and removing the real banana from the stalk.

Perform this casually, as though it is the most natural thing in the world for you to do. Peel back the skin and enjoy a snack.

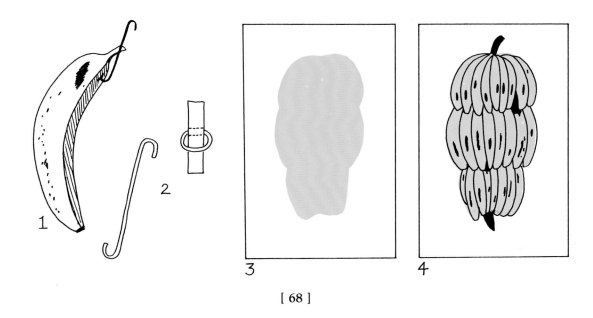

THE RISING CARD ♠

The Rising Card is a popular trick among many magicians. The magician asks someone in the audience to choose a card. Then he shuffles the card, mixes it back into the deck, places the cards in a glass, and on command causes the selected card to rise slowly out of the deck. Here is the same trick presented as a Chalk Talk.

This stunt takes a bit of planning. First, you need to prepare the card that will rise from the deck. The simplest way is to go to a magic shop and get a One Card Forcing Deck; that is, a deck in which all of the cards are the same except for one card that is on the face of the deck. So, whatever card is chosen is bound to be the one you want. Let's say, for example, that your deck is filled with the seven of spades. You will simply prepare one of them to rise in your drawing.

To do this, make a slit in the paper just behind the place where the top of the drawn pack will be. The slit should be large enough for a card to slip through.

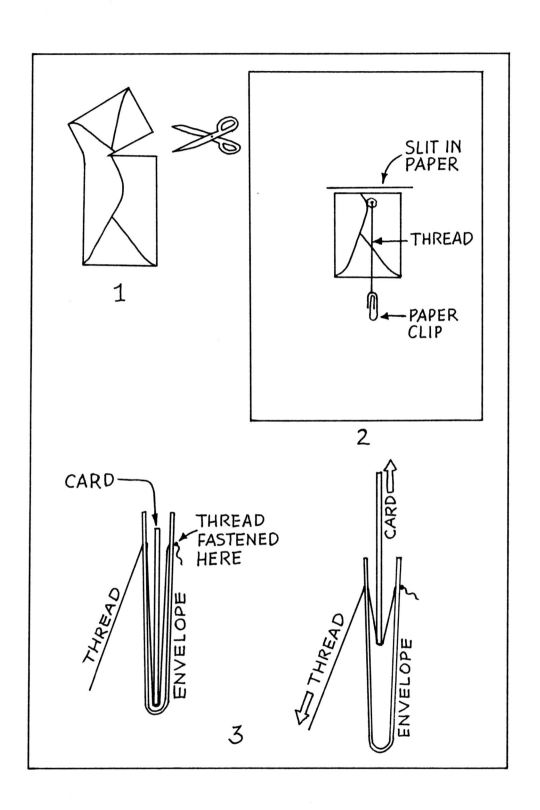

1

SLIT IN
PAPER

THREAD

PAPER
CLIP

2

CARD

THREAD
FASTENED
HERE

THREAD

ENVELOPE

CARD

THREAD

ENVELOPE

3

4

Find an envelope large enough to hold the real card. Close the flap and cut off one of the sides (see figure 1 at left). Paste the envelope to the back of the paper with its open side face up just below the slit. Leave a strip along the top free of paste.

Make a pinhole through both sides of the envelope near the top. Run a length of strong black thread through these holes from back to front. Fasten the thread with a knot. When the seven of spades card is pushed down into the envelope, the thread will be pushed down with it, as shown in figure 2. A pull on the thread will cause the card to rise out of the envelope (see figure 3). As the card rises behind the paper it will pass through the slit and appear to the audience to be rising from the pack in the glass.

To present the trick: Make a drawing of a deck of cards in a glass (figure 4). Take your One Card Forcing Deck and have someone select a card (since all of the cards are the same, the selected card will match the double that you have prepared).

Have the person call out the name of the selected card. As you stand beside your drawing board, pull on the thread and up rises the selected card from your drawing of a deck.

Remove the card and present it with a flourish to the person who chose that magical card.

The Pirate's Chest

This story of hidden treasure adds intrigue to your Chalk Talks. The basic elements of the story are shown in these drawings:

First a bag of money is removed from the drawn chest. Then a ghost rises from and descends back into the chest, and finally the pirate himself appears.

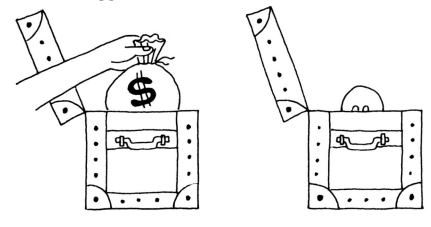

In preparing this trick, make a light pencil drawing of the pirate's chest. Next, make a slit in the paper where the top edge of the chest will be. See figure 1. Figure 2 shows you where to paste the large envelope on the back of the paper. The opening of the envelope, which you have to cut as you did in the Rising Card trick, should be just beneath the slit in the paper.

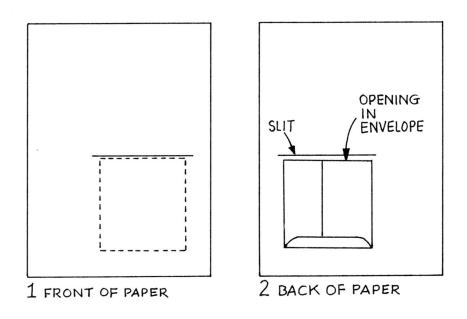

1 FRONT OF PAPER

2 BACK OF PAPER

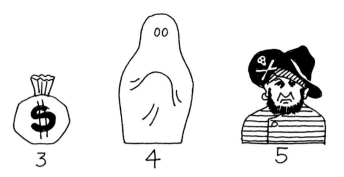

3   4   5

Draw the money bag, the ghost, and the pirate in black ink on cardboard. Draw them however you want to; you can even add some color. Make sure, though, that your drawings will fit into the envelope beneath the slit in the paper. Cut them out of the cardboard as neatly as you can. See figures 3, 4, and 5.

The drawings of the ghost and pirate rise from the chest by means of a thread attached to each one. Figures 6 and 7 below show how to do this, using the ghost as an example. It's very simple:

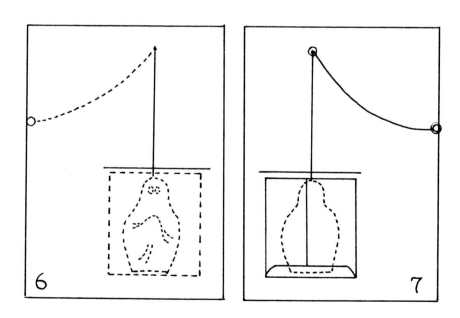

One end of the thread is attached to the ghost's head. See figure 6. By pulling on the thread you make the ghost rise out of the envelope, come through the slit, and appear to rise from the chest you have drawn on the paper. When you release the thread, the ghost sinks back down out of sight. A pull on the pirate's thread causes him to appear in the same way. When you put the cutout picture of the bag of money in the envelope, make sure it lies in front of the drawings of the ghost and pirate.

The lid of the chest is cut from the newsprint of your drawing pad. A thumbtack acts as a hinge so the lid can be raised (figure 8). Place a pin in the side opposite the tack to hold it in place. You will draw the chest itself on the drawing pad.

Draw a picture of the pirate's chest (figure 9) as you tell a sort of Treasure Island story. Add green chalk marks here and there to show the age of the chest and highlight it with orange.

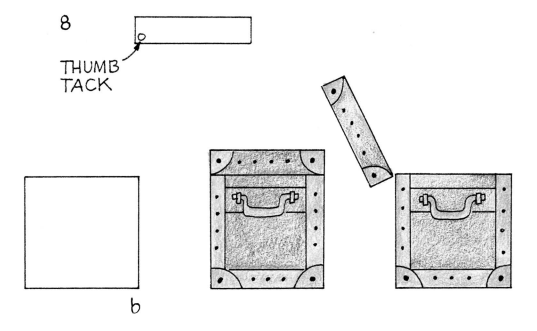

8

THUMB
TACK

9

When Harlan Tarbell did this magic trick, here is the story he told:

This is the treasure chest of Long John Silver. In it he hid his loot. When the old pirate died, his chest was discovered. The locks were pried off, and the lid was raised. [Remove pin and raise the lid on its thumbtack swivel.]

Inside the chest was a bag of gold. [Reach into your drawing of the chest by putting your thumb and forefinger through the slit. Bring out the drawing of the bag of money. Lean this against the drawing board on display.]

Suddenly there was an eerie sound, and from the chest a ghost arose. It looked around and then went back inside the chest. [Pull on the thread that will make the ghost rise up. When ready, simply release the thread, and the ghost returns inside the chest.]

Then with a shout [shout!] *the figure of Long John Silver himself arose, in spirit form.* [Pull the thread attached to the pirate drawing, and he slowly rises up.]

Long John roamed the seas for many years, searching for his treasure. Now it's time for him to rest with his gold nestled close beside him. [Release the thread and the pirate goes back inside the chest. Take the drawing of the bag of money and put it back in the chest, close the lid, and the story is over.]

And that's the story of Long John Silver as it was told to me. May he forever rest in peace.

FINALE
THE MAGICIAN'S RABBIT

For your finale, draw a cute bunny on white cardboard and cut it out as in figure 1.

1

Place the cutout bunny in a large envelope glued to the back of your drawing paper. Make a slit in the paper just above the top of the envelope pasted behind. This slit should be even with the rim of the top hat you are going to draw on the front of your paper. See figure 2.

Now, draw a top hat, as in figure 3. Reach into the hat and, through the slit, pull the cut-out rabbit from behind—it seems to come out of the hat in true magician style (as shown in figure 4).

Want to cause a sensation?

Have a LIVE WHITE BUNNY in a box offstage. After you pull the cutout rabbit from the drawn hat, have your assistant bring out the box and place the cardboard rabbit in it. *PRESTO!* You remove the real rabbit. Your audience will be dumbfounded.

This is the end of the show.

About the Author

Ormond McGill is a world-acclaimed magician who has been practicing his art for half a century. He has toured internationally with his stage shows East Indian Miracles and South Sea Island Magic.

His numerous books on magic include, for adults, *Entertaining with Magic, Atomic Magic, Psychic Magic*, and the *Encyclopedia of Stage Illusions*, and, for young readers, *Balancing Magic and Other Tricks, Science Magic: 101 Tricks You Can Do, Paper Magic, Voice Magic*, and *Mind Magic*.

A resident of northern California, Ormond tours, gives lectures, and does magic shows for children and adults.